CW00434537

identity theft

Everything you need to know
to protect yourself

IDENTITY THEFT

Copyright © Summersdale Publishers Ltd 2007

Text by Gavin Mills

Summersdale Publishers Ltd
46 West Street
Chichester
West Sussex
PO19 1RP
UK

www.summersdale.com

Printed and bound in Great Britain

ISBN: 1-84024-577-8
ISBN 13: 978-1-84024-577-6

Cover image © Shutterstock

identity theft

Everything you need to know
to protect yourself

Gavin Mills

summersdale

Contents

Introduction

What is identity theft and how does it work?

Identity theft has been around in one form or another for many years but today's technology is providing new ways for people to steal our personal information. Identity theft is one of the fastest growing crimes in the UK and a recent Home Office quote put the overall cost of identity fraud to the UK economy at a staggering £1.72 billion. The Credit Industry Fraud Avoidance System (CIFAS), the UK's fraud prevention service, estimates that identity fraud accounts for criminal cash flow of £10 million per day.

Estimates from The Association for Payment Clearing Services (APACS), the body that deals with fraud relating to bank and credit cards, reveal that all credit card crime has grown from £95 million in 1998 to £504 million in 2005. It is estimated that benefit fraud costs UK tax payers £3 billion a year, and identity fraud is a significant portion of this. Estimates from CIFAS suggest that in 2006 the number of victims of impersonation was up 19.1 per cent when compared with 2005.

These figures suggest that the criminals are one step ahead of the agencies and companies whose job it is to protect our data. Initiatives are being introduced rapidly to combat this new kind of crime but it's clear this is a problem that is not going away.

If your details are stolen and purchases are made in your name you are not liable for the debts incurred. However, apart from the headache which accompanies having to prove to the creditor the fact that it was not *you* who ran up these debts, lending institutions don't take these hits on the chin and chalk them up to the cost of doing business – they recoup their loses by increasing insurance premiums and interest rates, and raising service charges and the general cost of their products. Knowing how to protect yourself is vital to avoid the distress and inconvenience that comes with being the victim of identity theft.

Part One

What makes up our identity?

There are three basic elements to our identities:

Biometric identity

These are the physical attributes that are unique to an individual, i.e. fingerprints, voice, retina, facial structure, DNA profile, hand geometry, heat radiation, etc. Despite how much is made of the supposed infallibility of biometric identifying technology, the truth is that it is far from foolproof. In any case, at present this kind of technology is not in widespread use as a means of determining identity; it is really only of interest to governments and private industries concerned with protecting their research or worried about industrial espionage, as the equipment required is very expensive.

Attributed identity

This includes the components of a person's identity that are acquired at birth, including their full name, date and place of birth, and parents' names. Persons carrying out this kind of identity theft tend to be interested in the birth records of children who died in infancy.

Such situations are sometimes referred to as 'Day of the Jackal' identity theft, after Fredrick Forsyth's novel. However, determined thieves may not only target the records of children who die in infancy – there is nothing to stop a would-be identity thief from getting hold of *your* birth certificate as such documents are readily available from the Family Record Centre for a small fee. It is a public document so it requires no identification and the registrar cannot refuse a copy. These are known within the counter-fraud community as 'breeder' documents. Armed with such a document the thief can build on this foundation and apply for further forms of identification, as many institutions will use it to process an application – despite the fact that UK birth certificates contain the words 'a certificate is not evidence of identity'. Again, although popular in fiction and of great concern to the government since career criminals and terrorists might hijack identities and go untraced, this kind of identity theft is comparatively rare when seen alongside biographical identity theft.

Biographical identity

This type includes elements of identity which have built up over time. Identity theft of this kind is the most prevalent and causes the most difficulty and disruption to the victim. It will also be the focus of the bulk of this book. Biographical identity covers life events and how a person engages with structured society, i.e:

- registration of birth;

- details of education/ qualifications;

- electoral register entries;

- details of benefits claimed/ taxes paid;

- employment history;

- registration of marriage;

- mortgage account information/property ownership;

- insurance policies;

● history of interaction with organisations such as banks, creditors, utilities and public authorities.

Following legislation to combat money laundering in the UK, banks are now required to verify the name and address of new customers before opening an account. They achieve this by requiring the prospective customer to present two of the aforementioned documents as proof of identity and domicile. This leads to what the credit industry calls 'function creep': the function of certain documents 'creeps' into other areas. For instance, the function of utility bills is merely to tell you how much to pay your service provider, they are not identification documents, but in certain situations they are treated as bona fide credentials.

What do identity thieves do with the information?

Understanding how these criminals operate will help you to identify when you are most at risk and need to take extra precautions.

Identity fraud spans the criminal spectrum: from the opportunist who steals your credit card number and buys an iPod with it, to the running of sophisticated networks of illegal immigration, money laundering and drugs smuggling. It also encompasses frauds against the public sector by way of benefit fraud and individuals using false identities to avoid paying fines to the authorities. All of these criminals have something in common: they are attempting to hide their identity, their activities and their assets.

As stated earlier, biographical identity is by far the easiest to hijack. It is generally done by getting genuine government documents issued on the basis of false information (i.e. an identity thief may apply for a genuine driving licence using documents he has stolen from you) or by stealing genuine documents and forging the details contained on them.

Once an identity thief manages to acquire your information there are many ways by which he can carry out fraudulent activity. With just one piece of your identity he can obtain further identity documents which enable him to, for example:

- apply for a mobile phone contract in your name;

- apply for a credit card in your name;

- open a bank or building society account in your name;

- apply for other financial services in your name;

- apply for any benefits in your name (e.g. housing benefit, new tax credits, income support, job seeker's allowance, child benefit);

- apply for a driving licence in your name;

register a vehicle in your name; or

 apply for a passport in your name.

Obviously, once these items are in the thief's possession, he or she can run up huge debts using a credit or debit card in your name to make expensive purchases, or obtaining a loan with your details.

It may be hard to imagine a thief could wreak so much havoc with such little information as a starting point but, worryingly, this is not as impossible as you might think. For example, the UK Driver and Vehicle Licensing Agency (DVLA) will accept UK/EU/EEA passports (including travel documents issued by the Home Office) and EU/EEA national identity cards as means of identification for the purposes of obtaining a driving licence. Birth certificates (including adoption certificates) and foreign passports can be used but they must be accompanied by a photograph endorsed by a countersignatory – a non-relative who lives in the UK and has known the applicant for over two years. UK birth certificates state that 'a certificate is not evidence of identity' and the DVLA say that they *may* require further evidence. The reality, however, is that the DVLA only check a proportion of the countersignatories as the driving licence system is required by law to be self-financing. The DVLA is under pressure to keep cost increases to a minimum.

With a false driving licence in your name a car could be obtained on hire-purchase, as the signature on the card would match the one on the purchase agreement, and with an approved credit check the criminal could drive off in the car and, in an extreme scenario, sell it to *you* the next day. Thankfully, you will not be liable for the criminal offence of handling stolen goods, as you accepted them in good faith; however, this won't save you from the car being repossessed by the finance company.

The good news is that most identity theft can be prevented

with a little care in your daily routine. The following section will explain when you are most at risk and outline simple steps to prevent becoming a victim.

Part Two

How can I protect myself?

Identity theft is subject to the old adage 'an ounce of prevention is worth a pound of cure'. A minor change in how you manage your personal information could save you many sleepless nights and distressing phone calls and letters. Minimising your exposure to potential identity thieves does not have to involve fitting an impenetrable safe in the wall behind the family portrait, nor wiping your fingerprints off glassware in restaurants; it does, however, require certain extra steps to be introduced into your day-to-day life.

There are times in life when we are more vulnerable to identity thieves than others – it is on these occasions that a little extra vigilance will go a long way.

Theft of credit/debit cards

Situations under this heading comprise the most common types of identity fraud. Someone might steal your wallet, or even just one card from your wallet so you won't immediately know it is missing, and then use it posing as you. The chip and pin technology which is now in effect across the UK has had a significant impact on this type of fraud; however, if the fraudster already has your card they don't need your PIN to purchase goods online or over the phone as they are also in possession of your security code (the three digit number on the back of the card by the signature strip) for so-called 'card not present' transactions.

If you haven't noticed that your card is missing, the criminal is unlikely to be caught until the card reaches its limit and is declined. Even after the limit has been exceeded, the card can still be used for some time for smaller amounts which are beneath the 'floor limit' of shops, whereby no automatic check is made with the card company for the transaction. Then comes the phone call to *you* from the credit company.

To minimise the risk of this all too common occurrence, here are some simple safeguards:

- If you have cards you don't carry, keep them in a secure place and periodically check that they remain there

- Cancel cards that you no longer use: if the account is still active there is available credit to be stolen

- Keep your cheque book and cheque guarantee card in separate places

- If you have a high credit limit that you never use, consider requesting to have it reduced

- Examine your signature - if it is very easy to

forge you may want to consider changing it

- Don't choose an obvious PIN or store it somewhere it can be accessed by others

- Never let anyone see your PIN

All these tips apply both to credit and debit cards, but debit cards put you at greater risk as they often have your account number and sort code printed on the face of the card.

There is also the danger of your card details being stolen when you use your card in the normal way. This is called 'skimming'. It occurs where an employee processes your transaction but makes a copy of your details which they might use themselves for making purchases or sell on to a third party involved in fraud on a larger scale. That information can then be used in 'card not present' transactions, or might also be used to construct a fake credit card using your details.

Your funds can also be at risk even without your card ever passing into someone else's hands. Sophisticated thieves install equipment on the front of the card slot on an ATM which captures your credit/debit card number as you put it into the machine. Hidden above the machine is a miniature digital camera which captures the key strokes of you entering your PIN. All this information is then wirelessly transmitted to the thief's computer nearby. A card can now be created using all your data, thus enabling them to access your account.

More crude, but also very effective, is the use of the so-called 'Lebanese loop'. These are little slivers of film which are placed in the card slot, which trap your card when you insert it. Once it is stuck, a stranger approaches asking if you need help and more than likely telling you that their card got stuck the other day. They will probably suggest a series of steps for you to take, which will inevitably include you entering your PIN. Nothing you do will get the card back and once you leave in frustration, hoping to return during business hours to get your card from the bank, they pull out the Lebanese loop with your card in it and, having witnessed you entering your PIN, they now have all they need to access your account.

Credit card companies regularly monitor card usage and are likely to spot something that is out of the ordinary, the simplest example being recent transactions that are physically impossible: you purchase goods at your local supermarket and within minutes your account is being used to make a purchase in the USA

– this could be a case of 'skimming' and your card issuer should contact you to check. You won't be liable for the fraudulent purchase, but it will necessitate cancelling the card – this could be a real problem if you were travelling and unable to have a replacement card sent to you.

There are a few precautions which can reduce the risk of this type of scam:

- Be wary of how your credit card is being processed (suspicious delays, processing the card in another room). If you have a concern it is probably best not to challenge the vendor but instead contact your card issuer with your concerns right away.

- Regularly check your credit card/bank statements for anything suspicious - report any concerns to your card issuer immediately.

- If you must have multiple cards, consider designating

different cards for different types of purchases. This will help you identify any suspicious transactions.

— Notify your card issuer if you are travelling abroad – some specify that you must do this, but even if they don't, it's a wise move.

For information and tips on using your credit/debit cards safely see the Card Watch website at http://www.cardwatch.org.uk.

Moving house

Relocating is stressful and difficult at the best of times; there is no reason to add to your worries by making yourself an easy target for identity thieves. It is important that you inform all credit companies with whom you have a relationship of your change of address to minimise the risk of any sensitive information falling into the wrong hands. The Royal Mail offers a free service by which they take care of informing all your creditors and service providers of your change of address and over 1,000 companies participate in the scheme. If you would prefer to contact the companies directly, Royal Mail also offers a mail redirect service which will catch any that you forgot to inform of your new address and sent mail to your old one. Many people use this service for a short time to cover the transition period. See http://www.royalmail.com and follow the link for Customer Service. This service is definitely a good idea but it is not foolproof.

Your bank and credit card companies may know of your change of address, but offers of pre-approved credit cards or loans from companies unaware that you no longer live there may go out to your old address long after you have moved. An identity thief may accept such offers and incur debt in your name, or use the official documents received to authenticate other applications for credit.

To minimise your exposure to this type of fraud you should regularly check your credit file (see p. 96) as this will show all accounts still active at your previous address. You may also want to consider using the redirection service for up to a year and ensure that when you receive a piece of redirected mail, you contact the sender with your new address.

Extra vigilance should also be exercised if you live in somewhere which uses pigeon holes for holding your post – where others can have unfettered access to your correspondence it is imperative that you stay on top of things. If correspondence goes missing or you suspect it has been tampered with, get a copy of your credit report to see if there has been any unusual activity.

Travel

Travel poses its own risks to the security of our information. For instance, a discarded boarding-pass stub is a potential gold mine of personal information. If the boarding pass belonged to a frequent flyer club member it is likely that data can be gleaned from it. For instance, if the ticket was purchased with the relevant airline in the person's name using the frequent flyer number on the boarding pass, personal data such as passport number, nationality and date of birth would then be accessible. Armed with this information the savvy identity thief could then access public websites to find the person's address, which can then be used to source further documents. Care should always be taken when disposing of this kind of material: take it home with you and shred it before throwing it out.

Unfortunately, some disclosure of information is inevitable when you are travelling. Checking into a hotel provides a great deal of information about you: your address, telephone number, length of your absence from home, together with the credit card details which are often taken when checking in. Consider using your work address if such information is required when you register. It is also recommended that you use the room safe, if provided, or a safe provided by the registration desk, to keep your passport and other valuables safe during your stay. Granted this will not protect you from an unscrupulous hotel employee but it will save you headache should your room be burgled – your suitcase is not a secure place for these items. Similarly, if you are abroad and using a rental car you should be sure not to leave any valuables in the car when it is parked, *especially* identification and financial information.

As well as providing information on issues of concern in specific destinations, the Foreign and Commonwealth Office provides travel advice and tips for keeping your documents and money safe whilst travelling. See the 'know before you go' section at: http://www.fco.gov.uk/knowbeforeyougo.

Telephone calls

Identity thieves are a canny bunch and you may fall victim to their con by unknowingly giving your information away. People often ask for valuable information on the phone and they are not necessarily identity thieves – private investigators, sales people, pollsters and even police officers are all guilty of it. The identity thief goes a step further by taking that information and using it for wholly illegal purposes. It goes without saying that you should never give out sensitive information over the phone unless you are sure of whom you are talking to. But the fact remains that these are shrewd operators who use a number of very deceptive techniques to get what they want.

Seldom will an identity thief ask you for your banking details directly. More often than not they already have most pieces in the puzzle and are seeking the last one to give them access to credit in your name. The caller may already have your account number, sort code, address and date of birth and be able to cite them to you. Under the guise of a bank employee claiming a problem with your debit card, for instance, you are asked for the security code. Why would you suspect anything when the caller is already in possession of all that other information?

The rule of thumb here is to limit the amount of information you give out over the phone. All reputable creditors will go through a security check with you before asking for any sensitive information, which should go beyond just checking your address. You will generally be asked to give a specific digit in your password or PIN – NOT the whole thing – or a specific letter in your mother's maiden name – NOT the whole name. When in doubt, do not divulge any information and simply tell the caller that you will call back on the official number to go through the details.

A particularly audacious take on this con is when someone calls pretending to be from the bank and offers to sell you identity theft insurance. They will most likely already have the number of the credit/debit card that they are pretending to insure and only need the security code to give them unfettered access to your money. Once again, tell the caller that you will call back on the official number to go through the details. Your security code should only be divulged if you have made the call and you are absolutely certain of whom you are talking to.

You should be similarly wary of street canvassers – you may be stopped in the street by bogus canvassers and asked to take part in a 'survey' which involves divulging your personal details. Do not respond to their request for your details unless you are certain that they are legitimate, and even then be wary of giving more than one piece of information. For instance, don't give your address *and* your date of birth – most surveys will ask for you to give them an age range (i.e. are you between the ages of 18–25?) rather than an actual date of birth.

Bin bag theft

Debt collectors and private investigators have for a long time stolen bin bags that have been left out for collection in an effort to identify assets that can be seized by creditors. For identity thieves in the UK, this method of information collection is still in its infancy, but it is growing.

It is known as bin raiding in the UK and dumpster diving in the US. Typically these people are looking for documents or information that will enable them to piece together an identity: phone bills, utility bills, bank statements, credit/debit card receipts, employment and tax records.

Using stolen documents to obtain credit is certainly illegal, but stealing bin bags might not be deemed as theft if the thief could establish that he believed that it was abandoned property – even if the bag is in your rubbish bin he will have a defence to a charge of theft if he can show that he believed you had dumped the bag never intending to take it back.

The importance of shredding such documents cannot be overstated. Even seemingly safe information can be dangerous when taken in combination with other details. For instance, most credit/debit card receipts carry a line to show the card that made the purchase, but all numbers except for four are marked by an 'X'. The trouble is that not every system shows only the last four digits so it may in fact be possible to piece together your 16 digit number from various receipts.

- Shred all documents containing personal information before placing them in the bin/ recycling box.

- Consider disposing of some of the shredded paper at home and some at work.

Unfortunately, it is not only the rubbish from your home which is at risk of being raided – our employers possess all manner of sensitive information about us and it is vital that they take the responsibilities in respect of that data seriously. Companies which hold personal data have a duty of care under Data protection legislation to protect that information. You may wish to ask your employer what systems they have in place for disposing of confidential information such as payroll data, National Insurance numbers and tax information.

Sophisticated identity thieves no longer simply target the paper contents of your rubbish bin. The hard drive of any discarded computer is a potential source of information for the technically proficient identity thief. Deleting files on your hard disc is not sufficient to protect yourself – tools exist to recover files on a hard drive that has not been properly formatted. These programs are designed to assist us when disaster strikes our computer and we lose all our data. However, they can easily be turned against us. There are many programs that can help format your hard disc to reduce the chances of anyone lifting any data off it – consider the free program Eraser available at http://www.heidi.ie/eraser. However, it should be noted that none of the companies that produce such software guarantee that it is 100 per cent reliable. There are a few other options open to you:

- Find a local company, such as a machine shop, that will melt your hard drive – this method is secure but will probably incur a charge.

● Find a local company that will use a degaussing machine in order to eradicate your hard drive - the data is erased by generating a magnetic field which will make the contents of the drive impossible to reconstruct; it is a secure method but it will cost you.

● Use one of the programs mentioned above to format your drive, but run the program three to five times even if it states it's not necessary - this is

99.9 per cent secure but
it still remains possible
to recover data.

Deceased identity theft

CIFAS reports that impersonation of
the dead is the fastest growing form
of identity theft in Britain with a
year on year increase of 60 per cent.
Suffering the loss of someone close
to you is difficult enough without
having to deal with irate creditors
looking for money from your
departed dear one. Following these

simple steps should make a difficult
time a little easier:

● Don't include the date of
birth or address of the
deceased in any advertisement
announcing the funeral

● Notify government
departments (Department
for Work and Pensions,
HM Revenue) and return
any pension or allowance
books by registered post

● Notify any of the deceased's
creditors of the death

- When sorting through clothing to be donated be sure there are no documents containing sensitive information

- Don't dispose of any documents containing sensitive information without shredding them first

- Contact the Royal Mail to ensure that no one has set up a mail redirection service that you don't know about - this is especially important if the deceased's property is now empty

- Have a mail redirection service set up to forward post to your address – this is safer than collecting the post yourself

If creditors do contact you regarding debts in the deceased's name which were not theirs, explain the situation and also report the matter to the police and get a crime reference number. You should also contact CIFAS and get a protective registration against the deceased person's address – this can be done by a relative or executor of the deceased's estate – which will red-flag that address in case a credit application is made using it. For further information see http://www.cifas.org.uk. You can also register with the Deceased Preference Service, a free service which will remove the details of the deceased from the mailing list of many companies. For further information see http://www.deceasedpreferenceservice.co.uk.

Internet

The Internet has changed the way we communicate and opened up the world to us at the click of a mouse. However, like most technology it is a double-edged sword. It wasn't long before identity thieves struck upon the idea of using it as a tool to hijack our precious data. Extra caution is needed when communicating sensitive information over the net and an awareness of certain scams that have been in operation should help protect you from falling victim to them yourself.

If you are making any purchases online or doing any online banking it is imperative that you have an anti-virus programme and update it on a regular basis. It is also a good idea to install a firewall. These can be either software or hardware based (the home variety normally being software based) and operate to control and filter unwanted traffic going in and out of different zones, i.e. between your computer and the Internet. Once installed it runs constantly in the background so you don't have to set it up again. A firewall will ask for your permission to allow an application to access an outer network. You can deny this access if you don't want to send particular information over the network – this becomes very useful if your computer has been infected with a Trojan virus that will connect to other hosts and show them your keystrokes, giving them sensitive passwords or, worse yet, allowing them to take control of your computer remotely. In addition to these steps it's a good idea to download the latest security updates for your web browser and operating system.

Many websites require you to register your details with them so that when you return to make future purchases you don't have to re-enter you credit/debit card details. Ensure that in these circumstances you don't use an obvious password and be careful to logout properly when you have completed the transaction. When making purchases online it is important to ensure that you are giving your financial details over a secure webpage. Secured websites use encryption programmes to scramble your information as it is transmitted over the Internet. If the site is secure, the prefix to the domain address will be https://www. This can be found in the address bar.

Look also for a yellow closed padlock or an unbroken key icon at the bottom of your web browser.

If neither of these are present, consider discontinuing the transaction or enquire about alternative methods of ordering such as by telephone. It should also be noted that even if these secure indicators are present you should never use a public computer, such as one in an Internet café, to access sensitive financial information. For further information and advice on how to stay safe online see: http://www.banksafeonline.org.uk.

Phishing

A common technique utilised by the scammer is to send e-mails which when opened appear to be the website of your bank. They prompt you to enter your account number and password under the pretext that there is a problem with your account. The more advanced phishing pages will actually bring you to your bank's homepage once you have clicked 'login' after entering your information. By that point it is too late and they have your details. You may think that you would never fall for such a scam. Think again. In 2003 UK police estimated that phishing scams cost £60 million in the UK alone.

If you receive an e-mail that tells you there is a problem with your bank account and you must enter your details, delete the e-mail and contact your bank using a telephone number or website which you know to be genuine.

A notorious e-mail scam is the story of the wife of the late Nigerian head of state, General Sanni Abacha. The e-mail states that she has received $45 million dollars from a Russian contact which she needs to move out of the country and is willing to pay a 20 per cent commission to anyone who kindly provides their banking details for the transfer to take place. Targets have included companies, charities, churches and individuals. It may be obvious to you that it is a scam but it wasn't to the Brazilian bank manager who was hoodwinked out of $242 million. So widespread has this e-mail scam become that it has had a negative effect on foreign investment in Nigeria and they have passed criminal legislation specifically to combat it.

- Suspicious unsolicited e-mails of this kind should be deleted immediately.

- Never give your personal financial details to anyone by e-mail. Reputable companies would not request that you do this

as they understand that
it is not a secure method
of communication.

For regularly updated information on finance-related scams and swindles, see the following website created by the Financial Services Authority: http://www.moneymadeclear.fsa.gov.uk/scams.

Wireless surfing

The advent of wireless technology has allowed us to untie ourselves from our phone cables and surf the Internet anywhere with a hotspot. Wireless

Internet access is also becoming very popular in the home, allowing people to roam from room to room or numerous users to share the same network. Although very convenient, it does present certain security concerns that we should be aware of. An unsecured network makes it easier for hackers to access your computer. The following are some simple steps which should be taken to secure your wireless access:

- Every wireless router has a default username (a Service Set Identifier, or

SSID). Hackers interested in your personal information know what these are and with them can hack into your system. Your router's set-up instructions will tell you how to change the SSID to a different name.

- Enable Wired Equivalent Privacy (WEP) on your computer. WEP is designed to provide a level of security similar to that of a wired network. It aims to provide security by encrypting data over radio waves so that it is protected as it is transmitted from one end point to another. Windows XP is WEP enabled: you can set it to turn on automatically and it will prevent anyone snooping on your wireless broadband signal. For earlier versions of Windows, the WEP software should be included with your wireless network card/router.

When purchasing a wireless device, you might want to check that it is Wi-Fi Protected Access (WPA) enabled. This is a more advanced form of encryption than WEP and if your device has it you can simply turn it on by ticking 'Use WPA encryption instead of WEP' in the Wireless Network Setup Wizard.

These precautions should suffice for most homes; however, if you are handy with computers you could also consider more advanced security measures which will reduce even further the possibility of being hacked. Every wireless device has a Media Access Code, or MAC; this is a serial number that can be found on the outer casing of the device. You can enter the MAC address on each computer on your network and that will ensure that only those computers can access your wireless network. Your computer also has a MAC code, which you will need to get so that you can finish setting up the security measure. To find this, in Windows NT and later versions follow these steps:

- Click **Start, Run** then type **command** in the box and click **OK.** A new window will appear with a black background.

- Type **ipconfig/all** and press the **Enter** key. A list of information should appear in the window. Look for the line called **Physical address** - that's your computer's MAC address.

You will now need to input the MAC address to configure your router. Follow these steps:

- Click on **Start**, then **Control Panel** and then **Network Connections**

- In **Network Connections** right click on your wireless router icon and then click **Properties**

- Under **General** tab, click on the **Configure** button, then click on **Advanced** tab

- Under **Property** section, you will see **Network Address** or **Locally Administered Address,** click on it

- On the right side, under **Value,** type in the New MAC address you want to assign to your router

- Click **Start, Run** then type **command** in the box and click **OK.** A new window will appear with a black background

- Type **ipconfig/all** or **net config rdr** to verify the changes

⌐ Restart your computer

These steps initiate 'MAC address filtering' which means that your home wireless network will only work with devices that have the correct MAC codes.

Due to its very nature, wireless networking is not as secure as using a hard line to access the Internet. Nevertheless, these steps will increase the security of your network immeasurably and allow you to take advantage of the freedom which a Wi-Fi connection affords.

Part Three

How do I know if
I am a victim of
identity theft?

The importance of your credit report

If you want to ensure that you do not become a victim of identity theft it is vital that you become familiar with your credit report. Your credit report is a document which scores your credit rating so that lending institutions or service providers can decide if they are going to offer you credit or not. It contains the name of anyone you share a financial relationship with and also shows when you, or someone claiming to be you, have applied for credit and a lender has checked your file. Your report also contains linked addresses. A linked address is created when a lender changes the address on a credit account or when they receive a credit application from an address – if credit has been applied for in your name your report will contain all the addresses from which the application has been made. It is a good idea to order a copy and review what information lenders are seeing when you apply for credit.

Ordering a copy from one of the credit agencies is simple and costs £2. By law, the credit agencies (contact details are listed at the end of this book) are required to provide you with your report within seven working days of receipt of your request and payment. If you are concerned that you might be the victim of identity theft, you should request your report; however, more immediate action (contacting a lender or the police) may be necessary in extreme cases. The following are some signs to look out for:

- You have been unexpectedly denied credit even though you're sure that you're credit worthy

- Your credit/debit card statement includes charges which you don't recognise

- Your bank statements have not been delivered or you notice some other mail is missing

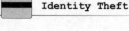

- A debt collection agency contacts you regarding a debt for goods you never purchased or credit you never took

- You are told that you are approved or denied credit for applications that you know nothing about

If you have ordered your report you should look for the following:

- Accounts in your name which you do not hold

●━ Credit applications made in your name which you did not make

●━ Searches of your report made by companies which you never contacted

●━ Linked addresses with which you have no connection

If you are concerned that some of the information held on your credit report is incorrect you can make an application to have the record amended. You can contact the credit agency who will then contact the lender who mistakenly appears on your report. Any amendments will be entered when the lender replies and take the form of a 'Notice of Correction' which can be viewed by anyone who has accessed your report in the past six months and it may influence their decision. If the information on the report suggests that you are the victim of identity theft, contact the relevant creditors immediately and explain your situation.

What to do in the event of identity theft

The most important thing to remember is that the problem will not go away if you do not take action and it will become harder to solve as time goes on. Do not ignore it. As previously stated, if you suspect your identity has been stolen be sure to order a copy of your credit report. If the report confirms your suspicions you should take the following steps:

- Contact one of the credit agencies listed at the back of this book and inform them of the problem. They can help you liaise with the lenders involved and make sure that you are not affected by the fraud. If the fraudster is still active they will place security features on your credit report.

- Contact the CIFAS Protective Registration Service. Once you have registered, CIFAS members such as lenders and banks will carry out extra checks whenever anyone, including you, applies for a financial service using your address.

●━ Report the incident immediately to the police and obtain a crime reference number or some other documentation as a record of the incident – for details on how to report crime see http://www.crimestoppers-uk.org/.

●━ When contacting your own lenders and the lender who was defrauded be sure to keep a record of communication – record who you spoke to and when and keep copies of letters sent and received.

Other steps to take:

- If your driving licence has been lost or stolen report it as soon as you discover it missing. For advice on what to do if your driving licence has been lost or stolen see: http://www.dvla.gov.uk/drivers.aspx.

- If your passport is lost or stolen report it as soon as you discover it missing. The Home Office has set up specific procedures to be followed in the event of lost or stolen passports. For further information consult the website at http://www.ips.gov.uk or call 0870 521 0410.

- Report all lost or stolen cheques, credit/debit cards to the issuers and request new ones. It is a good idea to follow up any telephone conversations you have with written confirmation. Once your new cards arrive you should immediately change your PIN – DO NOT continue to use a compromised PIN.

- If you suspect that your mail has been stolen or

a redirection has been fraudulently set up in your name, contact the Royal Mail and inform them of your concerns.

Your liability for the debt and how to deal with creditors

If you have been the victim of identity theft and purchases were made or credit advanced in your name it is important to remember that the debt is not yours. Most lending institutions limit your liability in the event of fraud to

£50 and even then it is common practice to waive such a fee.

There may be times, however, when you are contacted for an old fraudulent debt, about which you know nothing. A loan may have been advanced in your name some time ago and the creditor is now seeking repayment because the identity thief has made off with the money. They may be persistent as they are no doubt used to people denying their debts every day, but make sure that you are firm with them.

The process of collection will usually begin with a series of letters and then move on to phone calls – they probably won't turn up on your doorstep in the first instance. It will assist your case greatly if you are able to provide evidence of communication with the police and credit agencies to the effect that you have been a victim of identity theft. Sometimes, as with old debts, this might be impossible since the call from the debt collector is the first you will hear of the debt.

Remember: you have rights, so exercise them. If you find that the collection agency is acting unfairly then you should contact the lending institution which has retained them and inform them of the unfair practices. Guidance from the Office of Fair Trading makes it clear that lenders must not ignore the unfair practices of debt collectors acting on their behalf, whether in-house or external. Lenders should take care in the selection of third parties, investigate complaints and take action where appropriate. Failure to do so will call into question their own fitness to hold a credit licence. If a collector harasses you, you should contact your local council's trading standards department. If they threaten you physically, contact the police. If you start getting final demands for things you haven't bought, you can save yourself a lot of trouble by responding to them rather than ignoring them. Let the agency know that it's not your problem.

In the unlikely event that the process goes all the way to the bailiffs turning up at your door unannounced, there are some things you should remember:

— Bailiffs cannot enter your property by force unless they have been let in on a previous visit to collect the same debt. They can, however, make a peaceful entry which means they can enter through an open window or closed but unlocked door. You should always refuse to let the bailiff into your home as this will ensure that they cannot force entry if they visit again.

- Bailiffs cannot seize your basic household goods, clothing, bedding and tools of a trade. They are not allowed to seize goods belonging to a person other than the debtor but can normally seize jointly owned goods. The proceeds of any sale of jointly owned goods would have to be divided between the lender and the other owner.

Can I really make a difference in the fight against identity theft?

As illustrated by the figures at the beginning of this book, identity theft is on the rise. However, with a little extra vigilance on our part we can have a profound impact on those statistics and, indirectly, on the fees we pay to cover the cost of such fraud. Lending institutions and the government also have a role to play, but it is imperative that we act responsibly when it comes to controlling our personal information – we don't want to make it any easier for fraudsters to succeed. Identity theft is probably going to exist in one form or another for years to come; however, with a little effort you should be able to prevent yourself from becoming just another statistic in the fight against fraud.

Contact Information

Obtaining your credit report

You can obtain a copy of your credit report from the following organisations. Some also offer secure online access to your credit record for a small fee. Consult their websites for further details.

Callcredit
Consumer Services
Call Credit Limited
PO Box 491
Leeds
LS3 1WZ
Tel: 0870 060 1414
http://www.callcredit.co.uk

Equifax
Equifax Credit File Advice Centre
PO Box 1140
Bradford
BD1 5US
0870 514 3700
http://www.equifax.co.uk

Experian
Talbot House
Talbot Street
Nottingham
NG80 1TH
United Kingdom
0870 241 6212

http://www.experian.co.uk

Other titles available from Summersdale

geoff thompson

stress buster

how to stop stress from killing you

Stress Buster

How to Stop Stress from Killing You

Geoff Thompson

£7.99 P/B

ISBN: 1-84024-509-3

ISBN 13: 978-1-84024-509-7

In our increasingly hectic society we are under constant pressure to get the best results, the top job, a better car or a bigger house. For many reasons, stress can become a major problem affecting our relationships and even our health. Stress can ruin lives, and most people don't know how to cope with it – or how they can use it as an energy force.

If you're always getting angry in the car, at home or at work, if you constantly feel out of balance, then this book is for you. It will help you identify the causes of stress in your life, and shows you how to deal with them in a practical way. With true-life examples, clear explanations and relevant advice, it's indispensable aid to overcoming stress.

This book may save your life.

it's
easy being
green

Mark Mann

It's Easy Being Green

101 Ways to Save the Planet

Mark Mann

£3.99 P/B

ISBN: 1-84024-576-X

ISBN 13: 978-1-84024-576-9

This one-stop-shop of green tips on how to reduce, re-use and recycle will help make saving the planet easier. If you care about the environment and want to make a difference, these 101 tips will show you how.

Mark Mann is the author of *The Good Alternative Travel Guide* and edits and maintains environmental websites www.ecoshop.com.au and www.planetarkdirect.com.

THE BEGINNER'S GUIDE TO

broadband

AND wireless INTERNET

 Wireless Networks

Computer Security

Instant Messaging

Downloading Music

PC Phone Calls

Wi-Fi and Laptops

PETER BURNS

The Beginner's Guide to Broadband and Wireless Internet

Peter Burns

£5.99 P/B

ISBN: 1-84024-499-2

ISBN 13: 978-1-84024-499-1

If you're lost in cyberspace and need direction, this invaluable handbook includes all the information you'll need to get the most out of broadband. It guides you through the decisions you'll need to make, from choosing the right anti-virus software to setting up a wireless network in your home.

Learn how to make the most of your high-speed connection, with chapters on instant messaging, downloading music, making phone calls from your computer and finding the best broadband websites on the net. It's the book everyone with broadband needs next to their PC.

Peter Burns is the marketing manager (Internet and eCommerce) for retailer Waitrose and manages waitrose.com broadband, the UK's only broadband service to give all its profits to charity. He has also worked for Singapore Airlines, Virgin Atlantic and international news broadcaster ITN.

flying?
no fear!

conquer your fear of flying

Captain Adrian Akers-Douglas
& Dr. George Georgiou

Flying? No Fear!

Conquer Your Fear of Flying

Captain Adrian Akers-Douglas and Dr George Georgiou

£5.99 P/B

ISBN: 1-84024-527-1

ISBN 13: 978-1-84024-527-1

Written by an airline pilot and a clinical psychologist, this combination of practical explanation and self-help techniques is the definitive guide to help anyone overcome their fear of flying.

Sometimes unnecessary anxiety is caused by events which airline crews may take for granted, including aspects of flights that are mystifying and even alarming to less frequent flyers.

This new edition incorporates the recent advances in technology within the aviation industry, as well as the increased security checks as a result of 9/11.

Adrian Akers-Douglas started his career in the RAF, then flew for Cyprus Airways and Eurocypria Airlines for 30 years. Since 2003 he has been a check and training captain with Airbus, based in Toulouse. **Dr George Georgiou** is a clinical psychologist.

'a must for people who are frightened of flying'

Easyjet Inflight Magazine

www.summersdale.com